508.81
Hun   Huntley, Beth
         Amazon adventure

HILLTOP ELEM. LIBRARY
WEST UNITY, OHIO

Young Explorers

Amazon Adventure

Library of Congress Cataloging-in-Publication Data
Huntley, Beth.
       Amazon adventure.
       (Young explorers)
       Includes index.
       Summary: Describes the history of the Amazon River region, the plants, animals, and people that inhabit it, and its uncertain future in the face of rapidly encroaching modern civilization.
       1. Natural history--Amazon River Region--Juvenile literature. [1. Amazon River Valley] I. Johnson, Paul, 1951-   ill. II. Butterfield, Moira. III. Title. IV. Series: Young explorers (Milwaukee, Wis.)
QH112.H86   1989   508.81'1   88-42908
ISBN 1-55532-917-9

North American edition first published in 1989 by

Gareth Stevens Children's Books   *89-91*
7317 West Green Tree Road
Milwaukee, Wisconsin 53223, USA

US edition copyright © 1989. First published in the United Kingdom with an original text copyright © 1989 Victoria House Publishing Ltd.

All rights reserved. No part of this book may be reproduced or used in any form or by any means without permission in writing from Gareth Stevens, Inc.

Series editor: Valerie Weber
Research editor: Scott Enk
Cover design: Laurie Shock

1 2 3 4 5 6 7 8 9 94 93 92 91 90 89

Young Explorers

Amazon Adventure

Written by Beth Huntley
Illustrated by Paul Johnson

CONTENTS

Amazon Assignment 4
Journey Guide 6
Amazon Shopping List 8
Jungle Profile 10
Animal Life 12
Jungle Birds and Insects 14
Jungle Reptiles and Fish 16
Warning: Animals to Avoid 18
Jungle People 20
Mysteries and Legends 24
Early Explorers 26
Amazon Update 28
For More Information 30
Index 32

Gareth Stevens Children's Books • Milwaukee

AMAZON ASSIGNMENT

The Amazon is the second longest river in the world. Only the Nile is longer. It courses across South America from the Andes Mountains to the Atlantic Ocean. Hundreds of smaller rivers flow into the Amazon. Between them, they drain a massive area of land covering over 2.7 million square miles (7 million sq km). This area is the Amazon Basin, a vast wilderness of tropical forest and grassy plains.

American Indians have lived in the Amazon for thousands of years. Europeans did not explore the area until the 1540s, when Francisco de Orellana, a Spanish explorer, set out from Ecuador to explore the newly discovered South American continent.

When they got to the Atlantic Ocean, the explorers tasted the water. They were amazed to find it was fresh, not salty! It was fresh because the Amazon carries one-fifth of the world's fresh water, which flows from its mouth at millions of gallons each second. The fresh water pushes aside seawater and dilutes it for more than 100 miles (160 km) out into the ocean.

The Amazon is one of the richest wildlife areas in the world, but all of its jungle inhabitants depend upon each other for survival. Insects and small animals rely on jungle plants for food. Larger animals then eat these smaller creatures. If this food chain is broken, for example by people who destroy the forest plants, all the jungle inhabitants suffer.

The entire Amazon rain forest is being threatened with destruction. Find out more on page 28.

When the first Europeans arrived, they exploited and killed the Indians, stealing their land and forcing them into slavery.

People are still stealing Indian land today. Only a few Indian tribes remain. The ancient and unique skills of these people are dying out.

Before it is too late, we need to learn about jungle life from the Indians, and we need to find ways of helping these Indians survive. You can learn more about them on page 20.

European explorers named the Amazon area after a legendary tribe of women warriors called Amazons. Whether these women really existed is one of the many mysteries of this area. Learn about other legends on page 24 and about Amazon explorers on page 26.

5

JOURNEY GUIDE

The Amazon is about 4,000 miles (6,400 km) long and up to 150 miles (240 km) wide. It drains almost half of the continent of South America. No other river drains such a large expanse of land. If you were planning an Amazon expedition, you would first need to decide exactly where you wanted to go, since the Amazon covers such a huge and varied area.

The Amazon's beginnings are not in a single source but rather in hundreds of streams and lakes high in the Andes Mountains. The river starts about 100 miles (160 km) from the Pacific Ocean and then travels east, all the way across the continent. As the river gathers more water, it rushes in torrents and waterfalls strong enough to push boulders. A boat journey amid this pounding water would be impossible.

Manaus

As the river reaches level jungle, it slows down. By this time, it is carrying tons of mud wrenched from mountain ravines and ridges.
    Halfway along its length, it reaches one of the biggest cities in the Amazon region, Manaus. This city has a busy port filled with boats.
    Near Manaus, the muddy Amazon joins another huge river with clear water, the Rio Negro. For miles, the two rivers flow alongside each other between the same banks. But amazingly, their waters never mix, so it is easy to tell them apart.

In the lowland area, the temperature is hot and humid, with rain daily. Over 60 inches (150 cm) fall each year.

At times, the river bursts its banks, and water spills for miles into the jungle, flooding areas sometimes up to 36 feet (10 m) deep! When the jungle trees are in water, fish swim among them looking for food. You can paddle a boat between the trunks.

The Amazon River provides the best route into the jungle. Oceangoing ships can travel up the river to about 2,300 miles (3,700 km) from its mouth.

Beyond that point, the best way you can travel is by using a smaller boat. For centuries the Amazon Indians have used the perfect river craft, a lightweight canoe hollowed from a log.

Any expedition traveling along the river needs to employ some experienced navigators and jungle guides for help on the journey.

Belém

At the end of its course, about 4,000 miles (6,400 km) from its tumbling beginnings, the Amazon drops its load of mud and silt to form a group of islands in midstream. Such an area is called a delta. The Amazon has one of the biggest deltas in the world — one island is almost as big as the entire country of Switzerland!

The mouth of the Amazon at the Atlantic is huge — it is 180 miles (290 km) between the river's banks! At the mouth is the Amazon Basin's largest city, the port of Belém. It handles all the boats that sail up the river.

7

AMAZON SHOPPING LIST

The most important way you can prepare for an Amazon jungle adventure is to gather the right equipment. These pages show the vital explorers' equipment you will need to take.

You need a passport, plane tickets, and a money pouch you can wear under clothes. Be sure to get shots to protect you from disease, and pack medicine to ward off malaria, a disease carried by mosquitoes.

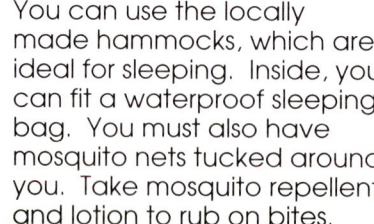

You can use the locally made hammocks, which are ideal for sleeping. Inside, you can fit a waterproof sleeping bag. You must also have mosquito nets tucked around you. Take mosquito repellent and lotion to rub on bites.
   You could take a lightweight, waterproof tent. Or you could sleep out in the open, under a canvas canopy.

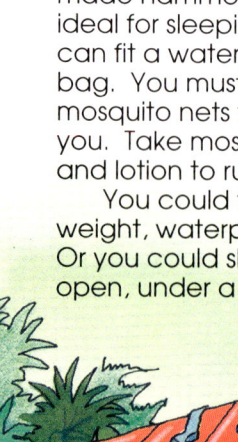

When it rains, keep yourself and your equipment dry under a hooded, waterproof poncho. You also need several changes of light, easily dried clothing.

Pack cameras and binoculars, as well as packets of silica gel to keep them from getting moldy in the humid air.

Take some thick plastic sacks to carry equipment. The Amazon people also use these sacks as raincoats.

You need a tough, inflatable boat to cope with the rapids, plus life jackets, helmets, ropes, and strong paddles, with a spare backup pair.

Take a camping stove, pots, and pans. You must first boil all water to kill germs and then add water-purifying tablets.

The Amazon Indians are usually very friendly and sometimes offer visitors food and shelter. You could thank them for their help with presents. Things they like but cannot get include hair combs and fishhooks. They like painkillers, too, as they tend to suffer from toothaches.

JUNGLE PROFILE

From the air, the Amazon jungle looks like a huge mass of almost identical green trees, but it is really made up of hundreds of varying species with many different animals living in them.

One good way to explore jungle life would be for you to climb a rope ladder to the highest branch of the tallest tree — that's about 200 feet (60 m) high.

On the way up, you would notice that the wildlife varies in each layer of the tree foliage. Different groups of creatures and plants live on different levels.

A thick layer of wet leaves over the thin soil layer makes the jungle floor slippery and soft. This leaf litter provides a good home for thousands of insects.

The trees spread roots along the ground and grow supporting buttress roots around their trunks. Indians kick these hollow roots to make a loud, booming noise. They send messages this way, as though beating drums.

10

**200 feet
(60 m)**

At this height you are in what is called the emergent, the area of very tall trees that stick out above the rest. Harpy eagles use these trees as nesting sites and lookout posts (see p. 14).

**115 feet
(35 m)**

At this level you can feel the sun and the breeze. Green, ropelike plants called lianas hang down. Animals climb up and down these. At flowering times, this layer will be a mass of brightly colored blossoms with bees and hummingbirds flying around collecting nectar.

**60-115 feet
(18-35 m)**

At this level you will pass many plants twined around tree branches. These plants have aerial roots that gather water by just hanging in the air. Monkeys can scoop up rainwater from bowl-shaped leaves on some

**50-60 feet
(15-18 m)**

As you look up from the ground, you will see millions of leaves that form a massive green umbrella. These leaves make up the canopy, which is divided into layers.

At this level, you will come to a layer of branches at the top of the smallest trees. Here you may see parrots flying around and perhaps a sloth hanging down from a branch (see p.12).

11

ANIMAL LIFE

You may have trouble spotting animals in the jungle because they are usually well hidden by leaves. But you can often hear them — their sounds can be deafeningly loud, especially at night. These pages show a few of the many interesting animals in the Amazon.

Many different species of monkeys live in the Amazon. The largest and loudest is the howler monkey. Its extremely large voice box helps it to increase the sound of its call, which carries for miles.

Troops of little squirrel monkeys scamper along branches. The babies cling tightly to their mothers' fur. You may also see spider monkeys hanging onto branches with the ends of their strong tails.

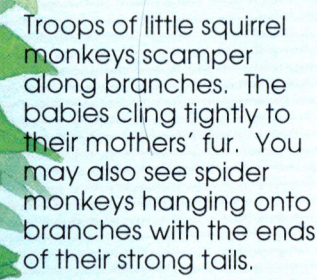

At night, bats use a built-in radar system to guide them. Amazon fruit bats also have a strong sense of smell, which helps them find ripe fruit.

Sloths move slowly and mainly live hanging upside-down in trees. Green algae often grow on their hairy coats and camouflage them so predators don't see them.

The furry tent-making bat prefers staying dry. It nibbles along the spine of a jungle leaf until both sides flop down. When it rains, the bat crawls under the leaf.

One mammal that lives in the Amazon River is the freshwater dolphin. Unlike sea dolphins, it is pink and almost blind in water. The river is so muddy that good eyesight would be useless.

Dolphins are intelligent creatures. They talk to each other in a language of clicks and chirps, noises that carry clearly under water.

Margay

The biggest Amazon cat is the jaguar. It prowls on the forest floor or sits on branches, waiting for prey to pass below. Usually the jaguar hunts land animals, but sometimes it stirs up the bottom of a pond with its paw to dislodge fish or dangles its tail in the water as bait to lure them.

Ocelot

The ocelot and the margay are both jungle cats with spotted coats that camouflage them. They are agile climbers. The margay — which hunts birds, lizards, and frogs in trees — can even climb down a tall tree trunk headfirst.

JUNGLE BIRDS

There are many hundreds of different birds in the Amazon rain forest. We will discuss some of the species you might see.

The scarlet macaw is actually shaded red, yellow, and blue. You may see it streaking through the jungle canopy, fetching food for its young.

A careful macaw parent will find a safe nesting hole in a tree trunk. The macaw can then enlarge the natural hole with its beak and rear its chicks inside, safe from any predators that might eat the nestlings.

There are many types of jungle hummingbirds. If you are lucky, you might see one hovering at the front of a flower, licking out the nectar. Hummingbirds are able to beat their wings up to 80 times a second. To get the energy they need to do this much work, they must eat every 10 to 15 minutes.

Scientists think the hoatzin bird looks a great deal like prehistoric birds in that the newborn chicks have claws on the ends of their wings. If they fall from the nests, the young birds use the claws to climb back.

The harpy eagle is the world's largest eagle, with feet the size of a human hand. It swoops down from high nests and grabs such animals as monkeys and sloths. The harpy itself is too big and strong for other jungle animals to catch.

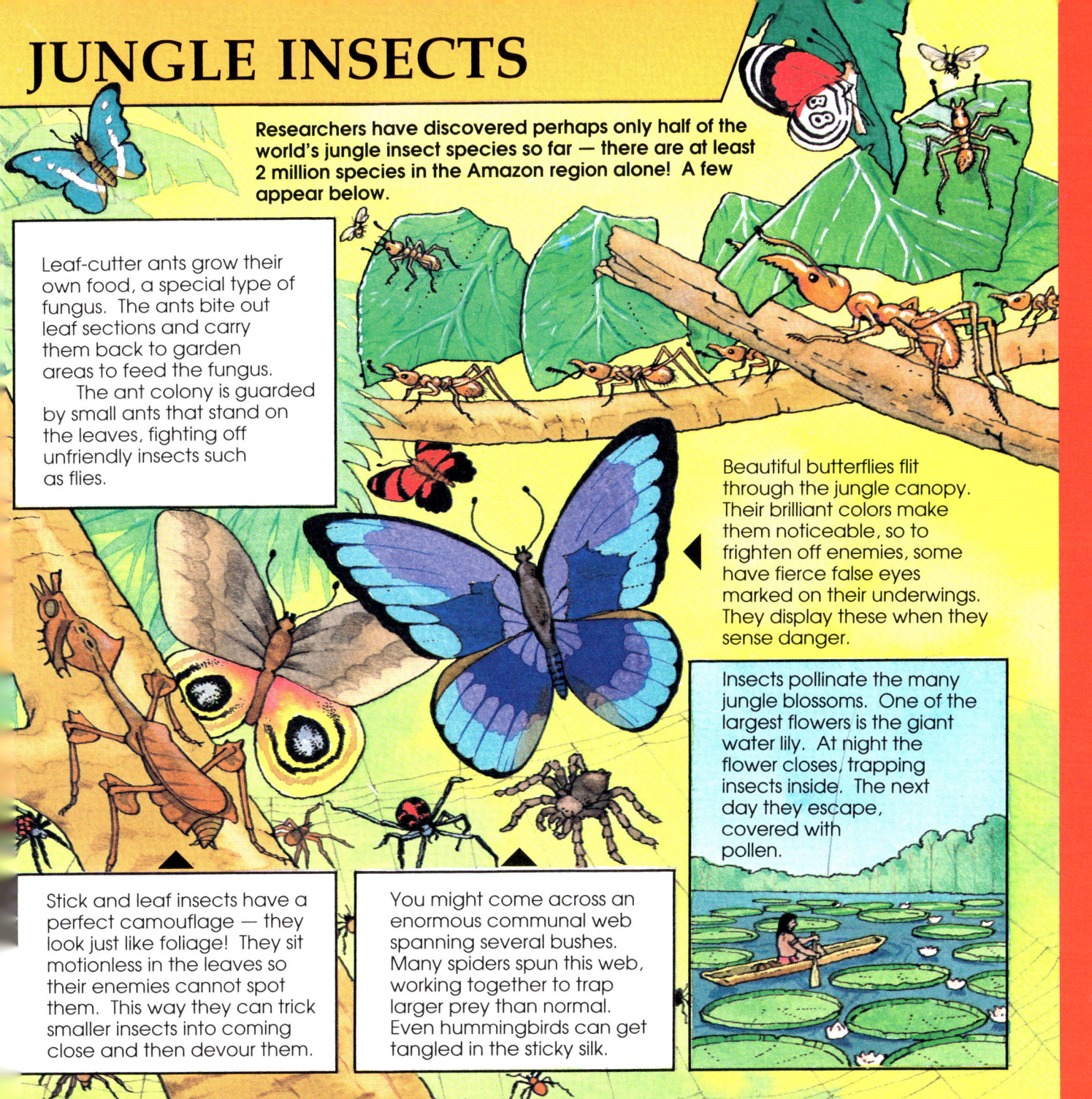

JUNGLE INSECTS

Researchers have discovered perhaps only half of the world's jungle insect species so far — there are at least 2 million species in the Amazon region alone! A few appear below.

Leaf-cutter ants grow their own food, a special type of fungus. The ants bite out leaf sections and carry them back to garden areas to feed the fungus.

The ant colony is guarded by small ants that stand on the leaves, fighting off unfriendly insects such as flies.

Beautiful butterflies flit through the jungle canopy. Their brilliant colors make them noticeable, so to frighten off enemies, some have fierce false eyes marked on their underwings. They display these when they sense danger.

Insects pollinate the many jungle blossoms. One of the largest flowers is the giant water lily. At night the flower closes, trapping insects inside. The next day they escape, covered with pollen.

Stick and leaf insects have a perfect camouflage — they look just like foliage! They sit motionless in the leaves so their enemies cannot spot them. This way they can trick smaller insects into coming close and then devour them.

You might come across an enormous communal web spanning several bushes. Many spiders spun this web, working together to trap larger prey than normal. Even hummingbirds can get tangled in the sticky silk.

15

JUNGLE REPTILES

Reptiles are cold-blooded, which means they cannot alter their body temperature. They have to rely on the sun to keep them warm, so the hot Amazon rain forest is an ideal home for them.

There are many jungle snakes, but most are easily scared away. The boa constrictor, one of the best known, can grow up to 18 feet (5 m) long. It eats small mammals and reptiles but in general it is harmless to humans. It kills its prey by coiling around it and squeezing it to death.

The green tree frog is one of the many jungle frogs that you can hear calling at night. Sticky disks on the tips of its toes help it to climb easily. It eats insects, leaping high into the air to catch them.

The basilisk is a small lizard that escapes danger by running quickly across the surface of the river on its back legs. Because it walks on water, some people call it the "Jesus Christ lizard."

Green iguanas can grow up to 6 feet (2 m) long. They are good climbers, with powerful toes for gripping branches.
Despite their fierce, dragonlike appearance, they are easily frightened. They will often escape danger by dropping down from a branch into the river. Using their tails, they swim quickly away under water.
Indians and Amazon travelers often eat iguana meat, which is said to taste like chicken. But the iguanas are agile and therefore difficult to catch.

JUNGLE FISH

There are over 2,000 species of fish in the Amazon region. A few are shown below.

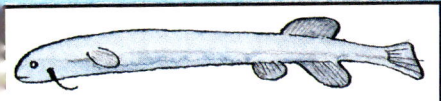

Some of the smallest fish in the Amazon River are bloodsuckers. One example is the candiru, which is only the size of a matchstick.

If it comes across a human swimmer, the candiru will swim into any opening in the body and wedge itself in with spines. It then has to be cut out by surgery!

River swimmers must wear tight-fitting swimsuits to keep this nasty creature out.

The pacu is a relative of the piranha, but unlike its flesh-eating cousin, it feeds on fruit that falls into the river. When the Amazon River floods, the pacu swims among the tree trunks, searching for food.

The electric eel has a unique way of collecting its food. It generates electricity and can deliver an electric shock of 650 volts to stun or kill its prey.

The arapaima is probably the biggest freshwater fish in the world. It can grow up to 10 feet (3 m) long and weigh up to 440 pounds (200 kg)! The Indians eat its dried flesh and use its rough scales as fingernail files.

The giant catfish can grow to be almost as big as the arapaima. It uses large feelers that look like whiskers to probe the riverbed for food.

17

WARNING: ANIMALS TO AVOID IN THE WATER

When you are traveling on the Amazon River, you must be on guard against dangerous animals in the water, lurking ready to attack. Keep a special watch for the species shown below, and avoid them at all costs.

The anaconda is the heaviest snake in the world. It can weigh as much as 500 pounds (225 kg) and grow to more than 25 feet (7.5 m) long.
    This snake often lies at the water's edge, waiting to ambush its prey, which it squeezes to death.

Be careful of stingrays if you step out of your boat onto a sandy part of the riverbed. Stingrays have flat bodies and hide in the sand. If a ray stings you, put vinegar on the wound to neutralize the poison.

If you see what looks like a rotten log floating in the river, watch out — it could be a crocodile! The Amazon crocodile, called the caiman, grows up to 15 feet (4.5 m) long. It will lie in wait for any land animal coming close to the edge of the water and will then attack with lightning speed.

Piranhas may be small fish, but they can be deadly. They hunt in groups and will attack any animal in the water, even people! Piranha teeth are so sharp that they can tear an animal to pieces in minutes. The Indians of the Amazon use the teeth as scissors.

18

ON LAND

Most Amazonian land animals are shy and will only attack if disturbed. Snakes and spiders tend to lurk hidden on the forest floor, so watch where you step. The following jungle animals are particularly dangerous to humans.

Be sure your mosquito net is always tucked in well because Amazonian vampire bats suck blood from the exposed parts of sleeping animals. The wound is not fatal, but the bats can pass on rabies, a deadly disease.

The bushmaster snake, which can grow up to 12 feet (3.6 m) long, is hard to see against jungle foliage because its brown skin camouflages it. Its bite can kill a person in a few hours.

This snake detects its prey by feeling body warmth. On each side of its head are heat-sensing organs.

The strongest poison made by any animal is produced by the arrow-poison frogs of the Amazon. A tiny amount will kill a human. The poison oozes from the frogs' skin, and Amazonian Indians sometimes use it on the tips of their arrows.

Tarantulas are among the world's biggest spiders — some grow bigger than the human fist! They usually feed on small reptiles, beetles, and birds.

Although humans do not usually die from the poison from these spiders, they can become very ill if bitten.

Scorpions like to creep into dark holes and warm places, so watch out for them in your equipment, especially in boots and bags. They can give you a nasty sting with their tails. Most scorpion stings are not fatal but they are quite painful.

JUNGLE PEOPLE

Before the Europeans arrived in South America in the 1500s, there were about 6 million Amazon Indians living in hundreds of separate tribes. Each tribe had its own land and customs.

Since that time, the lives of the Indians have changed completely, and their ancient skills are quickly dying out. There are now only a few hundred thousand Indians left.

The remaining Indian tribes live in small communities in jungle clearings. It is common for many relatives to live in one large communal house built from palm leaves.

The tribes organize themselves in different ways. For example, in some tribes there is a head man and a ruling council, while in other tribes, every member has equal rights and all the people in the tribe share their possessions.

The Jivaro Indians of Peru and Ecuador are one example of a surviving rain forest tribe.

The Jivaro have long had a reputation for being warlike — not only against outsiders but sometimes against each other. In the past, they would shrink the heads of enemies they killed in battle.

Now some Jivaro shrink the heads of animals such as sloths and monkeys.

Jivaro hunters remove the skin of the animal and shrink it by soaking it in a mixture of tree bark and water.

Then the skin is stuffed so it looks like a perfect miniature head, only a few inches high.

The Jivaro hang the heads outside their huts. Many tourists buy the shrunken animal heads as souvenirs.

Many Amazonian Indian tribes are skilled at hunting animals. Some use a blowgun, a straight hollow piece of wood over 6 feet (2 m) long. It shoots slender wooden darts tipped with a strong poison called curare, made from a woody vine.

If the hunter kills something small, such as a monkey, he will carry it home hanging from his shoulder. But it takes two people to carry a wild pig hung from a branch. When the hunter arrives home, the meat is chopped up, cooked, and shared.

When a hunter spots his prey, he takes a dart with a wedge of woolly material called kapok rolled around it and puts the dart into the end of the pipe. Then he aims the blowgun, which can weigh up to 10 pounds (4.5 kg), and blows. With one sharp puff, the dart can travel over 1,000 feet (300 m)!

Manioc

The Indians know where to find the edible plants that grow in the jungle. They also grow their own vegetables.

One of the most popular plants among the Indians is manioc. It looks like a long, thin potato. The Indians make manioc into a drink by peeling, boiling, and mashing it. Then they mix it with water and saliva and let it stand for several days.

The Indians usually have this drink at breakfast and at bedtime, often when they are lying in their hammocks listening to ancient tales. They may offer the drink to visitors.

21

JUNGLE PEOPLE — Continued

Getting food and drink in the jungle is not easy. When the Indians gather honey, they often have to dig it out from hollow trees. But there is a problem — the bees!

Rain forest tribes use the jungle trees in other ways. For example, they roll palm fiber into string and weave it into hammocks. They also use tree bark to make comfortable slings in which they carry their babies.

The Indians often plant chonta palm trees in their jungle gardens. The chonta fruit looks rather like a red peach, and it has a pleasant chestnut flavor when boiled.

The tree trunk is covered with spines, so the Indians plant a smooth-trunked cecropia tree next to each chonta. They can then climb this and reach across for the chonta fruit.

To decorate their faces and bodies, many Indians use homemade make-up. One source is the spiny achiote fruit. Inside it are lots of juicy red seeds. Many Indians squash the seeds to make a red paste that they paint on themselves.

Some Indians are very good at fishing. One easy way to catch fish is to make a fish poison by crushing the leaves of the barbasco plant to produce a milky paste. When this is poured into the water, it kills small fish and stuns larger ones. The Indians then just wade in to collect them.

International companies have long been mining the Amazon's minerals and have cut down its vast forests for their wood and for farmland.

Many Indian tribes have lost their homes and land. For many years, the law has made it difficult for them to fight for their land in the courts.

Another major problem is that the Indians have had very little resistance to illnesses brought in by outsiders. These diseases spread as deadly epidemics and have wiped out many tribes.

People have organized international projects to try to help the Indians survive. You can find out more about this on page 29.

MYSTERIES AND LEGENDS

Strange stories of monsters, lost explorers, and treasures still abound in the Amazon. The truth of these stories may never be known. Here are some of them.

In 1920 an Amazon explorer saw two huge monkeys screaming and brandishing tree branches. They were probably not gorillas, as no gorillas are known to live in South America. Other people have reported seeing giant apes in the jungle. Up to now, however, no one has photographed or captured one.

The legend of El Dorado is still perhaps the greatest mystery of the Amazon. It is said that El Dorado — the golden one — was a king so rich that he covered himself in gold.
 The king was said to swim each day in a lake high in the mountains. The gold was washed off, and the Indians threw more gold and jewels after it as an offering to their gods. Supposedly this treasure still lies hidden, though many have searched for it.

Somewhere in the jungle, a great, ruined city supposedly stands. In 1925 the explorer Percy Fawcett set out with two other men to find the ruins. They were never seen again.

Nobody knows what happened to Fawcett. Some say he was killed by Indians. Others say he lived the rest of his life in an Indian village.

Some Indians of the Amazon believe in many ghosts and monsters. Perhaps the most frightening of these is the Mapinguari, who is said to have one eye in the middle of his forehead.

They think this monster has a huge footprint and a body covered in hair. His scream is said to be so loud and strong that it can knock a human over with its force.

People have told many strange tales about mythical Amazonian tribes. Local Indians told some stories and early explorers made up other fantastic tales about what they saw. Some of these mythical tribes are listed below:
- a tribe of one-legged, hopping people
- a tribe of people that whistle through holes in their head
- a tribe of bat people who come out at night
- a tribe of people who are half-human and half-fish

One Amazon legend tells of a gentle jungle monster called the Caipora, whose feet are turned backward. He is supposed to look after the jungle animals and heal them when they are wounded.

The Caipora will punish any hunter who kills too many animals. He will lay false tracks so that the hunter gets hopelessly lost.

25

EARLY EXPLORERS

Since the Amazon was first discovered, adventurers have traveled there to find wealth, and scientists have come to study the people and wildlife of the jungle.

Early explorers were excited by Indian tales of treasure to be found in the jungle. Many searched for the city of El Dorado, where they hoped to find fabulous wealth.

In the 1500s, a Spanish soldier named Gonzalo Pizarro organized an expedition to find El Dorado. He took 220 Spaniards on horseback, 4,000 Indian slaves, and 2,000 pigs for food.

To pay for his adventure, Pizarro used treasure looted from other parts of South America.

The trip was a disaster. When the pigs had been eaten, the men ate their horses. When the horses were gone, they starved. In the end, only 80 Spaniards remained alive and Pizarro had to give up.

Many early expeditions ended in this same kind of failure because the Europeans knew so little about the jungle and did not have suitable equipment.

During his jungle expedition, Pizarro sent a party of men by boat down a river tributary to search for food. Leading the party was one of his men, Francisco de Orellana.

The men were swept into the Amazon itself and journeyed over 1,500 miles (2,400 km) through dangerous rapids and whirlpools, dense jungles, and plains until finally they reached the Atlantic. They were the first Europeans to cross the continent of South America.

In the 1800s, scientists began to come to the Amazon to study its varied wildlife and people. Three of the earliest visitors were the British naturalists Alfred Wallace, Henry Bates, and Richard Spruce, who took his dog, Sultan, on his travels.

These explorers spent years collecting and drawing species that had never been seen by scientists before. They contributed a great deal to our knowledge of the jungle.

Each man had some terrifying experience. For example, Wallace caught malaria on his journey. But luckily some Indians, who had never seen a white man before, took care of him. He once met a jaguar on a jungle path, and his gun was loaded only with useless birdshot. Again he was in luck — the jaguar merely gazed at him and then strolled on.

One famous visitor was U.S. President Theodore Roosevelt. His party took canoes down an Amazon tributary in 1914.

It was a difficult journey, with many rapids and whirlpools. Roosevelt became ill and some of his Indian guides were killed.

In the late 1800s and early 1900s, Europeans flocked to the Amazon to make their fortunes from rubber. Millions of rubber trees were tapped for their sap, and many Indians were taken as slaves to work the rubber plantations.

The Brazilian government made it illegal to export the rubber trees, but in 1876, British explorer Sir Henry Wickham smuggled many seeds to England to be germinated. The trees were shipped to Southeast Asia and a rubber business soon flourished there, which caused the Amazon trade to die.

AMAZON UPDATE

The Amazon jungle is neither as glorious nor as massive as it was when the early explorers arrived. Humans are rapidly destroying it, so the next few years may be your last chance to visit it before it is altered forever.

Other people have gradually driven the Amazon Indians from their old ways of life. They have dug up their lands for mines, cleared their lands for trees, or flooded their lands by building dams for hydroelectric power plants. When these dams are built, vast areas of the jungle are covered with water to create large lakes, and all the animals that live there are drowned. Conservationists argue that there is enough electricity in some of the areas where dams are planned, so further flooding is not necessary.

When loggers and farmers chop down the jungle trees, millions of animals die. Creatures such as parrots, jaguars, and monkeys cannot survive without their jungle homes, and some species are already disappearing. For instance, expeditions in the next few years may be the last to see a rare species of woolly monkey and some of the Amazon's most beautiful parrots.

Loggers fell other trees to reach the valuable mahogany tree, which is used to make fine furniture. They then leave these other trees rotting on the forest floor.

Loggers and ranchers are cutting down the Amazon forest at a rate of about 3.6 million acres (1.5 million hectares) every year — more than 15 square miles (40 sq km) a day! This forest cannot be replaced, and it is believed to provide much of the Earth's oxygen.

Although some tribes still live in the forest, many Indians now live on Indian reservations a fraction of the size of their original land. They are gradually forgetting the skills that once enabled them to live in harmony with the jungle.

International organizations are trying to help the remaining forest tribes by campaigning to get areas of land set aside for them.

It is important that the Amazon Indians survive and that we learn from them. They alone know the secrets of living in the rain forest, and they alone can teach us their unique skills and knowledge of nature.

29

FOR MORE INFORMATION

Magazines

Here are some children's magazines that have articles about the Amazon River and the surrounding region. If your library or bookstore does not have them, write to the publishers listed below for information about subscribing.

Dodo Dispatch
34th Street and Girard
Philadelphia, PA 19104

Elsa's Echo
3201 Tepusquet Canyon
Santa Maria, CA 93454

National Geographic World
National Geographic Society
17th and M Streets NW
Washington, DC 20036

Owl
The Young Naturalist Foundation
59 Front Street East
Toronto, Ontario
Canada M5E 1B3

Ranger Rick
National Wildlife Federation
1412 16th Street NW
Washington, DC 20036

3-2-1 Contact
Children's Television Workshop
One Lincoln Plaza
New York, NY 10023

Tracks
P.O. Box 30235
Lansing, MI 48909

Addresses

The organizations listed below have information about rain forests and the plant and animal species living there. When you write to them, tell them exactly what you want to know.

Forest Service
U.S. Department of Agriculture
P.O. Box 2417
Washington, DC 20013

Friends of the Everglades
202 Park Street, #4
Miami Springs, FL 33166

Books

The following books concern the Amazon River, its wildlife, and the surrounding area. If you are not able to find them in your library or bookstore, ask someone to order them for you.

The Amazon. Cheney (Franklin Watts)
Animals of the Tropical Forests. Johnson (Lerner)
Brazil. Cross (Childrens Press)
Brazil. Sherwood, ed. (Gareth Stevens)
The Jungle. Norden (Raintree)

Life in the Jungles. Richards (McGraw-Hill)
Looking at Brazil. Kendall (Lippincott)
Take a Trip to Brazil. Lye (Franklin Watts)
Tropical Forests. Jennings (Marshall Cavendish)
Tropical Rain Forests. Goetz (Morrow)

Glossary

Aerial Root
A root that does not start underground as most plant roots do but rather emerges from branchings on the stem of a plant. They gather nutrients and water from the air to feed the plant. Aerial roots low on the stem may reach the ground, forming *buttress roots*. Other aerial roots allow the plant to climb structures and other plants.

Amazons
Fierce women warriors from Greek mythology. They allowed no men to live in their society and trained their girls to be archers for war.

Buttress Roots
A system of roots that come from the trunk of a tree above ground. The buttress roots support a tree as ropes support a tent.

Camouflage
A way that animals conceal themselves from possible *predators* and from potential prey. The primary way animals camouflage themselves is through their color. Many animals are colored to blend in with their normal background. Some animals change their color with the season. Others, such as the chameleon, can change their color almost instantly to suit varying backgrounds. The cells in the skin pigment of the chameleon will produce more of whatever color it is sitting on.

Canopy
The overall forest roof of leaves and vegetation.

Curare
A deadly poison extracted from a plant. Curare has little effect when swallowed but when injected or applied to an open wound, it acts swiftly to paralyze an animal or person. Synthetic curare has been used to relax patients during surgery.

Emergent
A group of plants that rises above the mass of treetops or the forest roof.

Hydroelectric Power Plant
A facility that uses falling water to make electricity. The water can be from a natural waterfall or from an artificial dam in a river. The dam blocks the flow of a river and produces a lake with a high water level. The water can then fall from a great height to hit a turbine. The turbine spins magnets or coils of wire that generate electricity. One unfortunate result of the damming of a river to produce a lake is the flooding of large amounts of land. Wildlife and their homes are lost, as well as human dwellings, hunting grounds, and farms.

Nestling
A young bird while it is still in the nest. Usually young birds are hatched blind, naked, and helpless. The baby birds stay in the nest for some time and are completely dependent on their parents until they leave the nest.

Plantation
A large farm on which crops are raised, often by workers who live there.

Predator
An animal or person that lives by hunting, catching, or eating other animals.

Reptiles
A group of cold-blooded animals with backbones and covered with scales or horny plates. The body of a cold-blooded animal stays at the same temperature as its surroundings. This means reptiles cannot survive a wide range of temperature. Reptiles include snakes, lizards, and dinosaurs. There are 6,000 species of reptiles alive today.

Tributary
A river or stream flowing into a larger stream or river. The Amazon River has the greatest number of tributaries in the world — there are hundreds. Seventeen of the known tributaries are more than 1,000 miles (1,600 km) long.

Index

achiote fruit 22
aerial roots 11
Amazon Basin 4, 7
Amazons, the 5
anaconda 18
Andes mountains 4, 6
ants 15
arapaima 17
arrow-poison frog 19

barbasco plant 23
bats 12, 19
Belém 7
birds 11, 14, 15
boa constrictor 16
bushmaster snake 19

caiman 18
Caipora 25
candiru 17
canopy 11, 14, 15
catfish 17
cecropia tree 22
chonta fruit 22
climate 7
crocodiles 18
curare 21

dams 28
delta 7
disease 8, 23
dolphin, freshwater 13

El Dorado 24, 26
electric eel 17
emergent 11
Europeans 4, 5, 20, 26, 27

expeditions 6, 7, 26, 28
explorers 4, 5, 24, 25, 26, 27, 28
explorer's equipment 8-9

Fawcett, Percy 25
fish 17, 23
fishing 23
floods 7, 28
flowers 15
food, Indian 17, 21, 22, 23
frogs 16, 19

ghosts 25
guides 7

hammocks 8, 21
harpy eagle 11, 14
hoatzin 14
hummingbird 11, 14, 15
hunting 20, 21

iguanas 16
Indians 4, 5, 7, 9, 10, 19-25, 29
insects 15
international
    organizations 29
    projects 23

jaguars 13, 27, 28
Jivaro 20

leaves 10, 11
liana 11
lizards 16

mahogany 29
make-up 22

Manaus 6
manioc 21
Mapinguari 25
margay 13
monkeys 11, 12, 20, 21, 24, 28
monsters 24, 25
mosquitoes 8
mosquito net 8, 19
mysteries 24-25

ocelot 13

pacu 17
parrots 11, 28
piranhas 18
Pizarro, Gonzalo 26
plants 5, 11, 21, 22, 23
power plants 28

rain forest, destruction of 5, 23, 28
Rio Negro 6
Roosevelt, Theodore 27

scarlet macaw 14
scientists 26, 27
scorpions 19
slavery 5
sloths 11, 12, 14, 20
snakes 16, 18, 19
spiders 15, 19
stingrays 18

tarantulas 19
trees 22, 28, 29
tribes 5, 20, 23, 29